YOUNG

✳ ✳ ✳

THE COLOURFUL PERSONAL LIFE OF QUEEN VICTORIA

ILLUSTRATED WITH PORTRAITS FROM THE AUTHOR'S COLLECTION

SUSAN SYMONS

FASCINATING ROYAL HISTORY

Published by Roseland Books
The Old Rectory, St Just-in-Roseland, Truro, Cornwall, TR2 5JD

ISBN 13: 978-0-9928014-3-4
ISBN 10: 0992801435

For my daughter Frederica, who means so much to me, and who I have always thought should play Victoria.

CONTENTS

1

INTRODUCTION

My fascination with Queen Victoria began many years ago when, quite by accident, I found an old portrait of her in our attic. This portrait is shown as an illustration on the next page. It's not very exciting, but for some reason it took my interest; I put it up on the wall and I started to read up about her.

And what I found out astonished me. The overwhelming image we all have of Queen Victoria is as she is shown in this picture, which is from her golden jubilee year of 1887, when she had been fifty years on the throne. She is elderly, serious and unsmiling, even gloomy; more of a symbol than a person. My husband always calls this picture 'The Old Bag'. But Victoria has a colourful life story which is full of drama, intrigue and surprises.

So, I found a young princess who survived a damaging childhood possibly to save the monarchy when she came to the throne as a pretty eighteen-year-old. I found a married queen who in public projected the image of a model Victorian wife and mother, but who in private created endless scenes with her husband and actively disliked babies. And I found the elderly matriarch whose children and grandchildren spread out across the thrones of Europe, but who took with them the curse of haemophilia, bringing tragedy to families and contributing to the collapse of thrones. Above all I found a passionate and complex woman, who was loving and loyal; but also obstinate, self-centred, and controlling. The picture in the attic sparked my lifelong interest in Victoria's story and was also the start of what became my collection of portraits of her.

This is the first of three books about *The Colourful Personal Life of Queen Victoria*. For me her story splits naturally into three parts. This book is about the *Young Victoria* and looks at the first part of her life. It covers the somewhat bizarre circumstances of her birth, when there was an undignified race to produce the next heir to the British throne; her lonely childhood under a tough regime and without any friends of her own age; and the national adulation when she succeeded to the throne as a teenager. It ends with how she fell in love with Albert.

1. The picture I found in the attic – an elderly Queen Victoria in her Golden Jubilee year, after fifty years on the throne.

2. The young Queen Victoria as a teenager, at the beginning of her reign.

This book is a personal view of the story of *Young Victoria*, from many years of researching and reading about her. It is not a comprehensive account of Victoria's reign but instead focuses on her as a woman – her personal life, the events that formed her character, and the relationships that were important to her. I have used some of her own words, from her journal, to help tell the story; and there are more portraits and other memorabilia from my collection as illustrations. I have also included some charts and family trees at the back of the book which I think could be of assistance to the reader.

One of the reasons why Victoria is so fascinating is that there is so much to read about her. There are dozens of biographies, and these are still being written today; historians are always finding new things to say about Victoria. Even better there is a huge amount of original material. Victoria, herself, was a prolific letter writer and wrote thousands of letters, some of which have been published. She was also a talented diarist who wrote a daily journal for most of her life. Although this was doctored by her daughter Beatrice after her death, it still provides a detailed record of everything that happened to the queen and what she thought about it. The journal is in the Royal Archives at Windsor, but a special initiative of Queen Elisabeth II's diamond jubilee year of 2012 was to make it available online. So, if you want to, you can also read about Victoria in her own words, and form your own opinion of her.

Young Victoria is based on talks I give to branches of the Women's Institute (WI) in my home county of Cornwall. The ladies of the WI have been most supportive and encouraged me to write this book. It will be followed by two more – Victoria and Albert, about the middle part of her life and covering her marriage to and relationship with Albert, when they changed the image of the royal family and founded a dynasty; and The Widowed Queen, about the long years of her widowhood after Albert's early death, when she became the doyenne of sovereigns and the grandmamma of Europe.

3. Victoria as a child in a bonnet with ribbons.

I hope you will enjoy this book if you like history, or follow royalty, or are interested in people's personal stories. I have tried to make it light-hearted and easy-to-read. I wrote the book for the same reason that I give my talks about Victoria; because I want to share my view that history need not be a dull subject and that royal history is fascinating and fun. Royalty have always been the celebrities of their day and I think their stories from history can rival anything in modern-day soap operas.

Queen Victoria's journal

On 1 August 1832, thirteen-year-old Princess Victoria of Kent wrote the first entry in a small book, given to her by her mother. This began a habit of keeping a daily journal (or diary) which would last a lifetime. The last entry was made on January 13 1901, only nine days before Victoria died.

The queen seems to have been aware of the historical importance of her journal, and on her death she entrusted it to her youngest daughter, Beatrice, with instructions to edit it for posterity. Starting with the entries for 1837, when her mother ascended the throne, Beatrice began the laborious task of transcribing the journal. She amended or omitted anything she considered sensitive, and destroyed the original volumes as she went. It was a Herculean task that was not completed for nearly forty years.

Victoria's grandson, King George V, was not happy about the loss of what he knew were irreplaceable historical documents. However he felt unable to stop his aunt Beatrice since she was only doing what her mother had asked.

Only thirteen of the original volumes in Victoria's handwriting survive, covering the period before she came to the throne. They are followed by 111 volumes of Beatrice's work, covering the rest of Victoria's life.

2

THE ROYAL RACE FOR THE BRITISH CROWN

Queen Victoria was born on 24 May 1819 at Kensington Palace in London. Some of the first surprising things about her are that if it had not been for a national tragedy she would not have been born at all; she very nearly wasn't born in Britain; and her first name was not Victoria.

The national tragedy was the death in childbirth some eighteen months before of Princess Charlotte, the only child of George, prince of Wales. She died giving birth to a stillborn son. The prince of Wales would succeed his father as George IV in 1820 but already ruled as the Prince Regent, because George III had been declared mentally incapacitated. Charlotte was next in line to the throne after her father, and incredibly her death meant that there was no heir to the British throne in the next generation. I call this incredible because George III and his wife Queen Charlotte had fifteen children which had seemed sure to guarantee a prolific royal family and a multitude of heirs.

But this was not the case. When Charlotte died, the twelve surviving children of George III were all middle-aged, and most of them were unmarried. They had plenty of illegitimate children, but did not have a single legitimate child who was eligible for the British throne.

This was a national crisis as well as a tragedy. No one relished the prospect of the throne passing sideways between seven middle-aged brothers, followed by their five middle-aged sisters, and then off to a distant connection. So the death of Princess Charlotte sparked off an unlikely series of events that has been called *The Royal Race for the British Crown*. What happened was that those sons of George III who were still bachelors rushed about Europe trying to persuade German princesses to marry them, so they could father the future king or queen of England.

4. Princess Charlotte, heiress to the British throne, died in childbirth in November 1817.

Please see chart 1 at the back of the book which shows the ages and marital status of the seven surviving sons of George III at the time of the death of Princess Charlotte in 1817.

The choice of a German princess for these princes was standard at the time. There were simply more princesses to choose from in Germany than in any other country. It was not then a single country (as it became after World War I), but a patchwork of dozens of independent states each with their own royal family. This multitude of royal families is what made Germany the royal marriage market. Some of these states were tiny and their ruling families poor, but their daughters were of royal blood and therefore eligible. German princesses were selected to become queens and empresses and to fulfil the greatest roles in the society of their day.

Victoria's father, Edward Duke of Kent, was the fourth son of George III. When Charlotte died he was fifty years old, he was unmarried, and he was heavily in debt. He was living in Brussels because it was cheaper to live abroad than in England, and he was living with his mistress of twenty-eight years standing, a lady called Julie De St Laurent. The two were a settled and comfortable couple. But the Duke was tempted by the prospect of Parliament paying off his debts if he got married and fathered an heir. So he too proposed to a German princess, Victoire of Saxe-Coburg, and she accepted him. The only fly in the ointment was that he was fond of his mistress and could not bring himself to tell her about it; when she eventually did find out it was by reading in the newspaper that he was getting married!

5. Victoria's parents – Edward, duke of Kent;
and Victoire, princess of Saxe-Coburg.

To save money, Edward and Victoire were married in a double cere-mony at Kew Palace near London with his next older brother William, Duke of Clarence (the third son of George III), and his bride. This was another German princess called Adelaide of Saxe-Meiningen. Clarence had also previously lived with his mistress, Mrs Dorothea Jordan, for twenty years and had ten illegitimate children with her. She was a famous actress who had supported Clarence and their family from her earnings. But when her money started to dry up he dumped her and looked around for an heiress to provide the funding instead. When no heiress would accept his proposal, he too joined the *Royal Race*. It was fortunate that the new Duchess of Clarence was a kindly soul who accepted his illegitimate children and provided a home for them.

I mentioned that Victoria very nearly wasn't born in England, and this was again down to money. After their marriage, Kent and his wife returned to live abroad because it was cheaper, and when the duchess fell pregnant they couldn't afford the journey home. But Kent had a feeling about the destiny of his child and knew it was important that he or she be born on British soil. Although being born abroad could not affect the baby's legal place in the succession, it would make a great deal of difference to its acceptability and place in the affections of the British public.

Victoria's ancestry was, in fact, as German on her father's side as on her mother's. Only a hundred years before (in 1714) a German duke had taken over the British throne, when the ruler of the state of Hannover in Germany succeeded his distant cousin Queen Anne, and became King George I. As well as being the marriage market for princesses, Germany was also the market place for kings. There were many other examples where German dukes were chosen to be kings of European countries – including Russia, Sweden, Belgium and Greece.

George I was the first of the Hanoverian dynasty of Great Britain; and up until Victoria they were the monarchs of both Great Britain and Hannover. George I and George II were both born in Germany, spoke German as their first language, and much preferred Hannover to England. George III was the first Hanoverian king of Britain to be born in the country and to speak reasonable English. All of the Hanoverian kings were married to German princesses. Please see chart 2 at the back of the book for Victoria's parents and grandparents.

So that his child would be born in Britain, Kent appealed to his older brother, the Prince Regent, for money for the journey home. But there was bad blood between the two brothers, dating from quarrels many years before, and the Prince Regent refused. He was not very enthusiastic about this baby and may have been bitter because he was also young enough to father a new heir, had he not been saddled with an estranged wife he loathed. So the Prince Regent was difficult about his brother's coming child and seemed equally determined that the Kent baby would be born abroad.

In the end, some friends of Kent stumped up, and late in the day, when the duchess was already seven months gone, the Kents and their entourage set out from Germany. They travelled by coach and horses and Kent himself drove the coach as he did not want to take any risks with the duchess's delicate state. He drove at a snail's pace so that it took them nearly a month to reach Calais, where they crossed the English Channel. But they reached Kensington Palace in time, where on 24 May 1819 their baby daughter was born.

6. The room in Kensington Palace where Victoria was born.

But she wasn't the only royal baby that spring. As a direct result of the *Royal Race*, there were four of them. They were all born within a period of two months; they were all legitimate grandchildren of George III; and they were all eligible for the British throne. Chart 3 is a list of the four babies born in spring 1819, and their order, amongst each other, in the succession to the British crown.

Heiress to the British throne

In a hereditary monarchy, there are usually two types of heir to the throne. An heir apparent *is born the first in line to inherit the throne and can never be displaced from that position by the later birth of another person. For example, Charles, prince of Wales, the eldest son of Queen Elizabeth II, is the current heir apparent to the British throne.*

In contrast, Victoria was born the heiress presumptive *to the British throne. This means that she was the first in line to inherit in her generation, but would have been pushed down the pecking order by the later birth of a more eligible heir – if her parents had produced a son for example, or if any of her father's three older brothers had a child of either sex.*

In the event, Victoria did slip back when the duchess of Clarence (the wife of her father's elder brother) had a second daughter in 1820. But baby Elisabeth lived for only a few months and after her death Victoria was back in top spot. She was never again displaced and remained heiress throughout the rest of her childhood.

Although she was born third of the four babies in time, Victoria was the heiress from her birth. If her cousin Charlotte of Clarence (born on 27 March 1819) had survived, she would have outranked Victoria, because the duke of Clarence was the third son of George III and the duke of Kent the fourth. But little Charlotte only lived for hours and died the same day that she was born. The other two babies, George of Cumberland and George of Cambridge were behind Victoria in the order because their fathers were younger sons. Both these baby boys would have interesting lives. George of Cumberland became king of Hannover after his father, but was deposed, and his kingdom annexed by Prussia, after he chose the losing side in the Seven Weeks War of 1866. He spent the rest of his life campaigning (unsuccessfully) for the return of his kingdom and his fortune. George of Cambridge joined the

7. In this early portrait Victoria's status as heiress is indicated by the view of Windsor Castle in the background.

British army and rose to become commander-in-chief. He lived a long life, dying three years after Victoria in 1904.

Another surprising thing about Queen Victoria is her first name – which was actually Alexandrina. I said that the duke of Kent and his older brother, the Prince Regent, heartily disliked each other and there was another row over the new baby's name. Kent wanted to give his daughter one of the traditional female names of the royal family, such as Charlotte or Elizabeth. These were the first two names given to the latest little British princess, the daughter of William and Kate, born in 2015. But the Prince Regent (still being churlish about his brother's success in the race to produce an heir) vetoed these. He also refused to let them use the female version of his own name – he was George, she could not be Georgiana. The matter wasn't settled, and the baby was still nameless, when they all stood round the font at her christening.

There, with the duchess in tears, the Prince Regent was pressed for a name. Let her be called after her godfather, he said grudgingly – her

8. Victoria's first name was Alexandrina and this print, from the very beginning of her reign, shows her as Queen Alexandrina.

godfather was Tsar Alexander I of Russia. Royal babies were usually given strings of names, but the Prince Regent would only agree to one more – her mother's name, Victoire or Victoria. And so the baby was christened Alexandrina Victoria. For the first few years of her life she was known as 'Little Drina', although later on Victoria was used.

Alexandrina Victoria were both foreign and not English names at that time. There was a suggestion during Victoria's childhood that she should change her name to something more English, but this never came to anything. And when she came to the throne she took Victoria as her reign name. Just at the beginning there was some confusion about her name. In my collection I have a print, dating from the time of her accession, which shows her as Queen Alexandrina (see the illustration opposite and on the book's cover). What I like about this print, as well as the name that makes it unusual, is the complete contrast to the portrait which I found in the attic. This is the *Young Victoria*, fresh and energetic, rather than the gloomy and staid old widow. Victoria's public image was very different at the start of her reign than at the end.

3

THE KENSINGTON SYSTEM

Queen Victoria always said she had a very lonely childhood. Her father died when she was only eight months old. The family were economising by spending the winter away from London, in Sidmouth on the coast in Devon, when the duke of Kent caught a chill when out walking. He was known for his strong constitution but this time it was of no avail; he developed pneumonia and died on 23 January 1820.

His death left the duchess of Kent and her daughter in a precarious situation. The duke had been very heavily in debt and the duchess had to renounce any interest in his estate, on behalf of herself and her baby, in favour of his creditors. She was alone and penniless, in a strange country where she did not speak the language, and without any friends in the royal family. The duchess wanted to return to Germany and the Prince Regent, who became George IV on the death of his father on 29 January 1820, wanted her to go.

But fortunately the duchess got some good advice from her brother, Prince Leopold of Saxe-Coburg. Leopold had been married to Princess Charlotte (whose death had sparked off *The Royal Race for the Crown*) and was still living in this country as her widower. He told the duchess it was vital that her daughter, as the heiress, be brought up in Britain;

9. Little Drina was brought up in Kensington Palace in London.

and just as important, he provided the funds to enable them to stay. The duchess moved back to Kensington Palace; and that's where little Drina was brought up.

Uncle Leopold was a real father figure for the fatherless little princess and he continued to help her and her mother. But as he got over his grief at Charlotte's tragic death, he began to focus more on his own interests. The Saxe-Coburgs were an ambitious family, and having failed to become king consort of Great Britain, Leopold was now after a throne of his own. In 1831, he accepted the throne of Belgium, a new country that had just become independent of Holland. He left Britain and his support of his little niece would now be from a distance.

The duchess of Kent was a loving mother, but also rather a weak and suggestible woman. It was unfortunate that during Victoria's childhood the duchess came very much under the influence of the comptroller of her household, a man called Sir John Conroy. Sir

John had originally been the duke of Kent's equerry; after the duke's death he transferred to the duchess's household, where he gradually obtained considerable influence over her. Speculation at the time and since is that the two were lovers, but this has never been proved. What is clear is that she was under his sway and also felt that he was acting for the best.

Sir John Conroy was a highly ambitious man; he was also very able. He realised that it could not be many years before little Victoria came to the throne, most likely while she was still a minor. In that case there would need to be a regent; if the regent were her mother, then he, Sir John, could have considerable power. He saw himself as master of the

10. Little Drina aged four, dressed in a miniature version of adult clothes and wearing an enormous hat!

future queen of England. So he devised a system of upbringing to keep Victoria dependant on her mother, and to make the duchess the prime candidate for regent. It was called *The Kensington System*.

There were two aspects to the system. The first was a PR (or public relations) campaign to promote the duchess to the British public, with her daughter at her side. There were staged public appearances and, from when Victoria was a teenager, regular royal tours around the country. For me, the message of the campaign is clearly communicated in the gorgeous double portrait of mother and daughter shown opposite, dating from the early 1830s. Although it is Victoria who is the heiress, in the portrait it is her mother who takes centre stage.

11. The heiress to the throne visiting a cotton mill at Belper in Derbyshire.

12. A gorgeous portrait of Victoria with her mother, the duchess of Kent.

The second aspect of the Kensington system was to isolate Victoria and keep her away from any influences other than her mother. She was separated from the royal family and from the aristocracy. She was not allowed any contacts outside her own small circle at Kensington Palace. She was never allowed to be alone, day or night. She slept in her mother's bedroom, and her governess sat there with her until her mother came to bed.

Under the Kensington System, Victoria did not have friends. Sir John hoped she would be friendly with his own daughter, Victoire, who was a few months younger. But, although Victoria longed for company of her own age, she was not about to fall in with his wishes; she largely ignored Victoire and despised her. Victoria's only friend during her childhood was her half-sister Feodora; who was the daughter of the duchess by her first marriage (she was a widow when she married

21

the duke of Kent). Feodora was twelve years older than Victoria, but the two were very close throughout their lives. I think Feodora was Victoria's only real female friend. However, even Feodora was sent away

when Victoria was eight-years-old. She was married off in an arranged marriage, to a minor German prince. Fortunately it would turn out to be a happy marriage, but Feodora should have been able to make a better match with her close connection to the British court. Basically she was got out of the way. Her prince was not wealthy and so Feodora would be plagued with money troubles all her life.

And so Victoria turned for friendship to her dolls. She had a collection of over a hundred and thirty small wooden dolls

13. A drawing of Princess Victoria in the 1820s.

and made a list of them, each with a name and history. They were not her babies, as Victoria was never keen on these; they were adult dolls and her friends and confidants. Many of them survive today in the Royal Collection.

But Victoria was fortunate in her governess, a lady called Louise Lehzen. Lehzen was German and came to Britain initially as governess to Feodora. She was appointed to her role with Victoria because she was eminently qualified, but also perhaps because she was a foreigner and had no connections here. Sir John may have assumed that, because Lehzen was dependent on the duchess, she would do what she was told. But it did not turn out that way. And although he had previously got rid of members of the household who would not fall in with his plans,

Sir John failed to dislodge Lehzen, who won the backing of the king and Victoria's uncle Leopold.

Lehzen proved a true friend to Victoria, devoting her life to her and supporting her during her difficult childhood. I think it is doubtful that, without Lehzen, Victoria would have survived the Kensington System in the good shape that she did. She was rewarded with the little girl's affection, and later with a powerful role in the new queen's household when Victoria came to the throne.

There is a story about how the young Victoria found out about her destiny to be queen of England. The story is probably not true, or at least is much embroidered, as it was not written down until many years later (by Lehzen). The story goes that when she was eleven, Victoria found her name in a family tree in a history book (which had been deliberately left lying around), and realised that she would become

"I see I am nearer the Throne than I thought I was."

14. The twelve-year-old princess with her governess; a depiction of the moment when Victoria finds out how near she is to the throne.

queen after her Uncle William (William IV succeeded his brother, George IV, in 1830). Her response was serious and dedicated. 'I will be good' she is supposed to have said.

15. Riding a donkey in Kensington Palace Gardens.

As the years went by and Victoria grew nearer and nearer to her eighteenth birthday, Sir John Conroy became increasingly desperate. As heir to the throne, Victoria would come of age at eighteen (rather than the usual twenty-one) and would no longer need her mother as regent. He saw wealth and influence slipping through his fingers. With the hope of a regency over, he would be back to be just head of the duchess's household. The only chance was to get Victoria to commit in advance to giving him a position of importance when she became queen. So he and the duchess demanded that Victoria appoint him her confidential private secretary in charge of her affairs. As private secretary to the sovereign he would have a great deal of power. But this Victoria steadfastly refused to do, despite relentless pressure from them both over the weeks around her eighteenth birthday.

The king, William IV, was fading fast; but he knew what was going on at Kensington Palace and he was determined to

16. King William IV.

live until Victoria reached her majority. He was at loggerheads with the duchess over Victoria's upbringing and seclusion from court. With an illegitimate brood of his own, the king was used to children and had naturally hoped to see his young heiress at his court. Under the Kensington System, Victoria was kept away. In the days before her eighteenth birthday William IV offered Victoria an independent income and establishment of her own; she was forced to refuse this in terms dictated by her mother.

17. Victoria aged eleven, with sketchbook and pencil.

So the king had no desire to see the duchess as regent, and he just managed to stave this off. Victoria's eighteenth birthday was on 24 May 1837 and William IV died a month later on 20 June. Victoria was queen and Sir John Conroy's hopes were over.

One of the new queen's first actions was to order her bed to be taken out of her mother's bedroom. The two were estranged after Victoria became queen and it was not until several years later that they were brought back together by Albert. There is no doubt that the duchess loved her daughter very much, but she never understood her. That the Kensington System failed was due to the character of Victoria as well as to the support she got from Lehzen, and from her uncle, King Leopold of the Belgians. She was an affectionate child, but she was also very strong-willed, even obstinate. Sir John's mistake was that he did not attempt to win her affection, but tried instead to break her will. This he could not do. And in the process he alienated her from her mother.

Queen Victoria's siblings

Victoria was the only child of the duke and duchess of Kent. However, one of the less well known things about her is that she did in fact have two siblings – a half-brother and sister from her mother's first marriage.

Victoria's mother, then Princess Victoire of Saxe-Coburg, was married for the first time to Prince Emich Karl, the ruler of the small principality of Leiningen (today part of the German state of Bavaria). She was his second wife and there was an age gap between the couple. Victoire was seventeen when she married and her bridegroom forty. They had two children – Karl, born in 1804 and his sister Feodore, born in 1807.

Emich Karl died in 1814 and his widow remarried four years later – this time to Edward, duke of Kent. As with her first marriage, her bridegroom was much older. Victoire was thirty-one when she married for the second time; Edward was fifty. Their only child was Victoria, born in 1819.

Victoria had a good relationship with her half-sister, Feodore, but was less close to her half-brother, Karl, who she felt had been a supporter of the Kensington System during her childhood. Karl, who became the prince of Leiningen after his father's death, died in 1856. Feodore married Prince Ernst of Hohenlohe-Langenburg in 1828. This was another small German principality (today part of the state of Baden-Württemberg). After her husband's death, Feodore retired to Baden-Baden where Victoria visited her for the last time shortly before Feodore died in 1872.

4

THE FLOWER OF ENGLAND

The young Queen Victoria burst upon the scene. You might have thought that in those times her age and her sex would be against her, but actually it proved to be to the contrary. From the first, her dignity and self-possession impressed everyone around her. And because she was young, inexperienced, and female, she was forgiven some early mistakes.

The new queen was such a favourable contrast to her predecessors. When she came to the throne, the standing of the British monarchy was at a low. When Victoria was born, George III was still on the throne but was in the throes of his illness (porphyria). The image of his last years is of the old, blind, insane, king shut away at Windsor. George III was succeeded by his eldest son, the Prince Regent, who became George IV. Debauched and bloated, George IV was so unpopular that when he died his obituary in *The Times* said

> There never was an individual less regretted by his fellow creatures than this deceased king. What eye has wept for him? What heart has heaved one sob of unmercenary sorrow?[1]

George IV was succeeded by his brother – William IV, known as the sailor king. He was an improvement, but he was still elderly, unattractive and not very bright. On William IV's death, *The Times* remarked that he was

...not a man of genius nor of superior talent, nor of much refinement.[2]

After these three unappealing kings, Victoria was a breath of fresh air. (Please see chart 4 for the kings of Great Britain between Victoria's birth and her succession to the throne.)

The events of her first day as queen are part of her legend. This is what she wrote in her journal

18. The new queen; a print published on the day of Victoria's accession.

for that day (the underlining for emphasis is Victoria's own)

I was awoke at 6 o'clock by Mama who told me that the Archbishop of Canterbury and Lord Conyngham were here, and wished to see me. I got out of bed and went into my sitting room (only in my dressing gown) <u>alone</u>, and saw them. Lord Conyngham then acquainted me that my poor Uncle the King, was no more, and had expired at 12 minutes past 2 this morning and consequently that I am <u>Queen</u>.[3]

That scene has been depicted in many Victorian prints, one of which is included in this book on the opposite page. Victoria is shown as young, innocent and female, dressed all in white, and is in such contrast to the elderly statesmen who have come to give her the news.

And of course, it is significant that she is on her own – there is no duchess of Kent in the picture, and no Sir John Conroy.

Victoria started as she meant to go on. During that long first day she received her ministers, held audiences and attended her first Privy Council meeting, always on her own. Only at the end of the day did she go to say goodnight to her mother, the duchess of Kent.

The impression she made at her first Privy Council on that first day was just tremendous. None of the men there had expected to see such dignity and confidence in an eighteen-year-old girl. The duke of Wellington, who was there, said

She not merely filled her chair, she filled the room.[4]

19. Victoria receives the news of her accession.

The famous diarist Charles Greville was also present in his official capacity and he wrote

> Never was anything like the first impression she produced, or the chorus of praise and admiration which is raised about her manner and behaviour, and certainly not without justice. It was very extraordinary, and something far beyond what was looked for.[5]

20. The impression she made at her first Privy Council, on the first day of her reign, was tremendous.

There was huge public interest in the new queen and the new reign was launched on a great wave of enthusiasm. Not since the death of Princess Charlotte twenty years before had there been a member of the royal family with whom the nation could identify.

Victoria was never a beauty, but at this stage of her life she was slim and pretty. The newspapers of the day were full of her. They emphasised her youth and potential, compared her to Elizabeth I, and portrayed her as the hope for the future. She was also celebrated in the street ballads, which were written to commemorate all the major events of the day. Here is the first verse from a street ballad, printed a few days after Victoria's accession. It is called *Our new Queen: The Flower of England* and is sung to the tune of a famous sea shanty, *The Roast Beef of England*, which you can Google and listen to on the internet.

> Come all you bold Britons and list to my rhymes
> Very soon alterations we'll see in the times,
> Happiness and prosperity soon may we find
> Here's a health to our young Queen Victoria,
> Victoria for ever, Huzza![6]

Street ballads

Ballad singers were a common sight on the streets of London in early Victorian times. They eked out a living by singing popular street ballads about topical events. In those days newspapers were expensive and mostly read by the better-off and educated. For the poorer parts of society, who could not afford newspapers, street literature and ballads provided both the news and the entertainment of the day.

A street ballad, sung to a well-known tune, could be written, printed, and circulated, in not much more than an hour. They were pasted on walls, sold at a cheap price, and performed by the ballad singers. Street ballads were commentaries on the times, and they were often ribald. Here's a verse from one called 'The Royal Marriage', published when Victoria married Prince Albert in 1840.

> Prince Albert's the man,
> Who will do what he can,
> That he'll please her will quickly be seen,
> For he'll make a quick passage,
> For a cargo of sausage,
> As a present for our young Queen.[7]

21. The Royal Rose of England, in a Spooner's Transformation.

Victoria's name and image were everywhere and the analogy to a flower was common. As part of my collection I have an interesting piece of ephemera which is a *Spooner's Transformation*. It's called *The Royal Rose of England*; it looks like a picture of a rose with Windsor Castle in the background, but hold it up to the light and the transformation occurs – it turns into a portrait of Victoria.

The new queen was crowned a year after her accession, on 28 June 1838. Because of Victoria's immense popularity the government decided to spend a massive £200,000 on her coronation. This was nearly four times as much as was spent for her predecessor, William IV. Crowds of up to a half a million flocked into London to see the show, which included a procession to and from Westminster Abbey, illuminations and fireworks, and a fair in Hyde Park.

22. Original invitation to Victoria's coronation in Westminster Abbey.

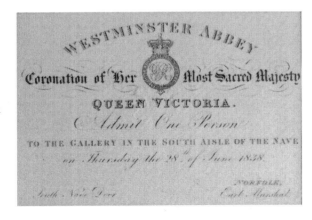

23 The nineteen-year-old queen, in her coronation regalia.

Victoria herself was astonished by the multitudes that turned out to cheer her procession. She wrote in her journal that the coronation was the proudest day of her life.

> Their good-humour and excessive loyalty was beyond everything, and I really cannot say <u>how</u> proud I feel to be the Queen of <u>such</u> a <u>Nation</u>.[8]

But, unlike British ceremonial today (which is immaculate), there was no rehearsal for the five-hour coronation ceremony, which took place in Westminster Abbey, resulting in some big gaffes on the day. No one seemed to know the correct order of service; they got into a complete muddle at one point when they turned over more than one page and thought the service was over! The queen retired to a side room and then had to come back again to finish the service off. There was another incident when the Archbishop forced the coronation ring on Victoria's wrong finger, nearly making her cry out in pain! It was made for her little finger but he forced it on the ring finger. Before she could leave the abbey she had to bathe her hand in ice-cold water for a long time to reduce the swelling and get the ring off. But the most remembered moment of the coronation was when an eighty-two-year-old peer (Lord Rolle) fell over as he was about to pay homage to the new queen. She charmed everyone by getting up off the throne and coming to meet him, to prevent him falling again.

24. The coronation ceremony in Westminster Abbey.

I said that Victoria benefited from her youth and inexperience and was forgiven some early mistakes, when an older male monarch might not have been. There was a genuine desire among her ministers to nurture and protect her. But the most serious of her mistakes occurred on the first change of government of her reign, when she refused to follow the accepted political practice.

25. A new father figure - the queen and Lord Melbourne
out riding at Windsor Castle.

When she came to the throne Victoria had confirmed Lord
Melbourne (the leader of the Whig Party) as her prime minister, on
the advice of her Uncle Leopold. Lord Melbourne was fifty-eight years
old, the widower of the notorious Lady Caroline Lamb, and very much
a man of the world. He was charmed by the innocent little queen and
Victoria, who was always looking for a father figure to replace the
father who had died when she was a baby, was equally delighted by
him. Her diary is full of affectionate references to him. Unfortunately,
under his tutelage she became an ardent Whig, even though the crown
was supposed to be above politics.

So, when Melbourne's government fell in May 1839, Victoria was
totally dismayed. She burst into tears on hearing the news and her
journal suggests that she wept for days. She was extremely reluctant
to accept the Tory leader, Sir Robert Peel, as her new Prime Minister.

She was uncooperative with him and adamantly refused to make any changes to her Whig-dominated household or to appoint any Tory ladies. Eventually, Peel told her that without her full confidence he could not form a government and Melbourne returned to power. Victoria was jubilant, but it was a serious error. In time she came to understand this and when Melbourne's government fell again in August 1841 she accepted Peel with better grace.

26. A cartoon about the *Bedchamber Crisis*, when Victoria refused to dismiss any of her Whig ladies.

But by the politicians of the day, her stubborn refusal to give up Melbourne or to follow accepted political practice was put down to feminine caprice, and the pressure increased on her to marry and to come under a husband's guidance.

5

ALBERT ... IS BEAUTIFUL

There were a number of reasons why it was thought that Victoria should marry as soon as possible. The first, already referred to, was that no-one thought a teen-aged girl could properly fulfil the role of a monarch.

> ... at an age at which a girl can hardly be trusted to choose a bonnet for herself; yet a task is laid upon her from which an archangel might shrink.[9]

It was expected that she would suffer from women's whims and shirk from the work involved, preferring lighter amusements. So it was important that she have the guiding hand and support of a husband.

Next, there was also the need for Victoria to have heirs as soon as possible and secure the succession. No one liked the parallel with Queen Elizabeth I here – a great queen, but one who died unmarried. Until Victoria did have children, the heir to the throne was her father's next brother down, the duke of Cumberland. He was a much-hated man in Britain – suspected of incest with his sister and possibly guilty of the murder of his valet. Cumberland had already succeeded as king

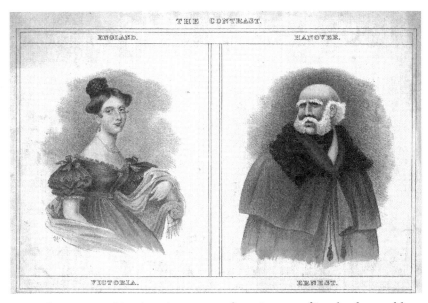

27. *The Contrast*; this Victorian cartoon from *Spooner of London* favourably compares Victoria to her uncle, the duke of Cumberland.

of Hannover, where Victoria could not take the throne, but nobody wanted him as king of England. A single life (Victoria's own) between Cumberland and the crown was just not enough. The feeling in the country is summed up by the Victorian cartoon shown on this page. It's called *The Contrast* and that's what it shows – the contrast between England on one side, in the person of a young and fresh Victoria; and Hannover on the other, with the elderly and unsavoury Cumberland.

And finally there were worries about Victoria's private life. After all, she too was a Hanoverian and they were notorious for what I might call their hot blood and their low morals. So, as long as she was not married, there was always a danger that she might be compromised or form an unsuitable attachment. This had nearly happened to Princess Charlotte before her marriage when she had to own up to secret meetings with a certain Captain Hesse.

The Salic Law of Succession

The Salic Law of Succession is the rule by which females and their descendants are excluded from succession to the throne in certain monarchies. The law originated in France, but also applied in some other countries. When William IV died in 1837, the rule did not apply in Great Britain but was followed in Hannover, with the result that the union of the thrones of these two countries (which had existed since 1714) came to an end. Victoria, who was next in line by birth, succeeded to the throne of Britain. As a woman however, she could not succeed in Hannover where the throne went instead to her uncle, the duke of Cumberland.

28. The young queen charming senior politicians from both the main parties of the day – the Whigs and the Tories

So even before Victoria became queen, there was a great deal of manoeuvring about when she would marry, and about whom she would marry; and there were different candidates for her hand. King William IV wanted her to marry a prince from one of the other major European powers, to cement diplomatic relations. He favoured one of the princes of Orange, grandsons of the Dutch king. But her mother, the duchess of Kent, wanted a prince from her own family – the Saxe-Coburgs. Prince Albert was the duchess's nephew, the son of her older brother Ernst. Albert was three months younger than his cousin Victoria and from his birth the Saxe-Coburg family had been planning for them to marry. The family tree in chart 5 explains the family relationship between Queen Victoria and Prince Albert.

29. The Saxe-Coburg candidate for Victoria's hand – Prince Albert at four years old.

The Saxe-Coburgs were only the rulers of a minor duchy in Germany and the British royal family considered them to be pushy upstarts. William IV was incensed that that the duchess of Kent should try to frustrate his plans over Victoria's marriage and the relationship between them, already poor, deteriorated further. There was a scene at a gala dinner for the king's birthday when, in his speech, William IV accused the duchess of keeping his niece away from court and said he would not stand for it. Victoria burst into tears and the duchess had to be persuaded not to order her carriage immediately, but to stay overnight for the sake of appearances. The situation was made worse because there was also bad blood between the Saxe-Coburgs and the

Dutch royal family over a previous royal wedding. Princess Charlotte had been engaged to a prince of Orange but had jilted him and married the duchess of Kent's younger brother, Prince Leopold of Saxe-Coburg. In spring 1836, when Victoria was still only sixteen, the king invited the two young princes of Orange, William and Alexander, to come on a visit with their father, with the intention of bringing about an engagement. The duchess immediately retaliated and invited her brother to bring his two young sons, Ernst and Albert. Both pairs of boys came within in a week of each other and were paraded in front of Victoria - but there was no engagement. Perhaps Victoria was influenced by her Saxe-Coburg relatives when she said she found the Orange boys plain and dull. She liked her Saxe-Coburg cousins better, but she did not at this stage fall for Albert.

30. Dressed for the evening; the young Victoria loved late nights and parties.

He was also only sixteen, still very much a boy, plump and unremarkable, and did not yet have the good looks that he would have a few years later. Unlike Victoria, who loved late nights and parties, Albert needed his sleep and couldn't keep awake after nine o'clock at night! The family decided that he needed to mature more before any plans could come to fruition and he was sent off on a grand tour of Europe.

Victoria understood that Albert had been selected as her husband by her mother's family – and in theory she accepted this. However, she saw it all as hazy and in the future, and after she came to the throne she was in no hurry to marry. She was enjoying her new life too much to give up her independence. At this point she denied to the family that she had ever given any promise to Albert and said that she did not consider herself bound to him. This was all very difficult for Albert, who had been trained from babyhood for the career of marrying Victoria. He was naturally anxious not to be kept dangling on a string while other eligible princesses in Europe were snapped up.

31. After she came to the throne Victoria enjoyed her new life and independence; dancing at a ball.

But there was one factor which did push Victoria in the direction of marriage and that was her ever worsening relationship with her mother. In Victoria's eyes, she was plagued by her mother with demands for money to pay off her debts, and with requests for honours for the Conroy family, to whom the duchess had remained loyal. As an unmarried girl, Victoria was bound to live with her mother and the only way she could live separately, without causing scandal, was if she got married.

32. Young Victoria in 1838.

Things came to a head in spring 1839 when a major scandal erupted at court about one of the duchess's ladies-in-waiting. Lady Flora Hastings had a swollen stomach and there were rumours that she was pregnant. Perhaps blinded by her hatred of Sir John Conroy, Victoria unfortunately added to these rumours, suggesting that Sir John could be the father.

It was a massive scandal. Matters reached such a pass that Lady Flora's family was forced to come to her defence publically in the press, and Lady Flora herself had to undergo something that was almost unprecedented for ladies – a medical examination without any clothes on. At that time, ladies were examined by doctors through their clothes; they did not remove them. The examination vindicated Lady Flora. Not only was she found to be a virgin, but she had an undiagnosed medical complaint. It was terminal and she died only months later, in July 1839.

Sir John Conroy

Sir John Conroy came from the minor Irish landed gentry. He made his career in the British Army, rising to be a captain in the Royal Artillery, helped by the patronage of his father-in-law, Major-General Fisher, who was a friend of the duke of Kent. After his father-in-law's death, Conroy was rather at a loose end. The duke was then setting up a new establishment in anticipation of his marriage, and Conroy joined his household as an equerry. (An equerry is a military officer in the service of a royal person.) Conroy was in attendance at Sidmouth when the duke became ill, and after the duke's death, he took charge of the duchess's household.

We cannot be sure about the nature of the relationship between the duchess and Sir John. Possibly it was platonic. The duchess seems to have been the type of woman who needs a man to lean on; there had been a similar relationship with a member of her household when she was the widowed princess of Leiningen. But the rumours that she and Conroy were romantically involved started soon after she was widowed, and have persisted ever since. The duke of Wellington suggested that the reason Victoria hated Conroy so much was that she had witnessed 'familiarities' between him and her mother.

After Victoria became queen, she refused to give Sir John any position in her household. He did not accept defeat with good grace however, but hung on with the duchess, making extravagant demands for a peerage, and a pension, in recognition of his past service. Anxious to be rid of him, Victoria's ministers compromised, agreed to a pension, and gave him a baronetcy (a baron is entitled to be addressed as 'Sir' but ranks well below a peer, who is addressed as a 'Lord'). But still Sir John stayed on in the hope of something better, and it was not until two years later that he resigned his position with the duchess and went to live abroad.

Years later, very large discrepancies were found in the duchess's accounts and it is likely that Conroy diverted significant amounts of her money for his own use. He was unrepentant to the end – still claiming on his deathbed that he had done the right thing by the duchess and her daughter.

Victoria's reputation was damaged by this affair. Either way she was tarnished – had Lady Flora had been pregnant there was immorality at court; as she was not, there was intrigue. And the affair did nothing for Victoria's relationship with her mother, the duchess of Kent, who, understandably, had sided with her lady-in-waiting and against her own daughter. Desperate now to live separately from her mother, Victoria began to think more favourably about marriage.

But who to marry was the question? She had a mild flirtation with a peer, but had to agree with Lord Melbourne that it would not do to marry a subject as this would only cause jealousy among the aristocratic families. Her two royal cousins, also born as a result of the *Royal Race*, were also crossed off the list; George of Cumberland because he was blind, and George of Cambridge, because at this stage of their lives

33. Windsor castle, where the cousins, Victoria and Albert, met again in October 1839.

he and Victoria did not much like each other. George of Cambridge greeted her eventual engagement with great relief. He never made a dynastic marriage, but later married an actress, whom he always claimed to have met on the queen's wedding day. The available foreign princes were discussed, but no one seemed to quite fit Victoria's bill. It kept coming back to Albert, but she was adamant that she could decide nothing until she had seen him again.

So, on the evening of 10 October 1839, the twenty-year-old queen stood at the top of the staircase at Windsor Castle to receive Prince Albert and his family. This was such a pivotal moment in her life; it would decide her whole future. All her doubts and fears just fell away the moment she saw him. She wrote in her journal

34. Prince Albert at the time of his marriage.

It was with some emotion that I beheld Albert, who is beautiful.[10]

For Victoria it was love at first sight. In the three and a half years since their first meeting, Albert had matured to become an extremely handsome young man. She was swept off her feet.

Albert really is quite charming, and so excessively handsome, ... a beautiful figure, broad in the shoulders and a fine waist. My heart is quite going.[11]

She made up her mind almost immediately and only five days later, on 15 October, she invited Albert to a private meeting where, in view of their relative positions (she was a sovereign and he a lesser ranking prince), she proposed to him (rather than the other way around) and was accepted. Victoria was ecstatic and poured out her heart in her journal.

... oh! to feel I was, and am, loved by such an Angel as Albert was too great delight to describe! he is perfection; perfection in every way, – in beauty – in everything! I told him I was quite unworthy of him and kissed his dear hand, – he said he would be very happy 'das Leben mit dir zu zubringen' [German for to share life with you], and was so kind, and seemed so happy, that I really felt it was the happiest brightest moment of my life, which made up for all I had suffered and endured. Oh! how I adore and love him, I cannot say!! ... I feel the happiest of human beings.[12]

6

VICTORIA AND ALBERT

Victoria and Albert were married on 10 February 1840. Their marriage would turn out to be a success. It would have its problems and would often be stormy, particularly in the early years. But perhaps this is not surprising given their different characters and expectations from this marriage.

For Victoria, Albert was a lifelong passion. She was totally devoted to him, but she was not easy to live with. She could be emotional, obstinate and self-centred. For Albert his marriage was his career and his temperament was more cool, logical and Germanic. Victoria was prone to make scenes. Albert would then retreat from her, wait until she had calmed down and then try reasoning with her in writing. And in the early days too, Victoria saw Albert as something of an ornament. She was reluctant to share her responsibilities or to give him a role. This was frustrating for Albert, who had been trained from babyhood to share the queen's workload and help her with her duties. But as time went by, she came to rely on him more and more; Albert took on the role of teacher and Victoria the willing pupil.

Their marriage worked and together they formed a new model of constitutional monarchy, (that we still recognise today); completely

changed the moral tone and public image of the royal family (to be completely different than the Georgian era before it); and founded a dynasty. They had nine children together who, through their own marriages, spread across the thrones and the royalty of Europe. So, in a way, with her marriage to Albert, Victoria's story was only just beginning.

35. Victoria and Albert were married on 10 February 1840.

Part 2 of The Colourful Personal Life of Queen Victoria

'Young Victoria' is the first of what will be three books about 'The Colourful Personal Life of Queen Victoria'. The next book will be 'Victoria and Albert', about the middle years of her life, when she was married to Prince Albert. This part of Victoria's story will show how the marriage of Victoria and Albert was against the odds and was very unpopular with the British public. It will look at early troubles for the couple, with power struggles, personality clashes, and unwelcome pregnancies, but also how they came through these to create a true partnership and a happy family life. And it will end with the story of Albert's death, and how a man in the prime of his life was worn out by the stresses and strains of being Victoria's husband.

CHARTS AND FAMILY TREES

1. The crisis over the lack of heirs to the British throne: the ages and marital status of the seven surviving sons of George III at Princess Charlotte's death in 1817.
2. Queen Victoria's German ancestry: her parents and grandparents.
3. The royal race for the British crown; the four babies born in spring 1819, showing the dates of their birth and their order in the succession.
4. Victoria's predecessors: the kings of Great Britain between the time of her birth and her succession to the throne.
5. The family relationship between Queen Victoria and Prince Albert.

1. THE CRISIS OVER THE LACK OF HEIRS TO THE BRITISH THRONE

The ages and marital status of the seven surviving sons of George III at Princess Charlotte's death in 1817

George, aged 55 married 1785 (secretly) no children?
Prince of Wales Maria FitzHerbert

married 1795 (dynastically) one child,
Caroline of Brunswick Princess Charlotte
1796 - 1817

Frederick, aged 54 married 1791 (dynastically) no children
Duke of York Friederike of Prussia

William, aged 52 unmarried 10 illegitimate children
Duke of Clarence by Mrs Jordan

Edward, aged 50 unmarried
Duke of Kent

Ernest, aged 46 married 1815 (dynastically) no children yet
Duke of Cumberland Friederike of Mecklenburg-Strelitz

Augustus, aged 44 married 1793 (secretly) two children (not royal)
Duke of Sussex Lady Augusta Murray

Adolphus, aged 43 unmarried
Duke of Cambridge

The dukes of Clarence, Kent and Cambridge
were all married (to German princesses) in 1818

2. QUEEN VICTORIA'S GERMAN ANCESTRY
- HER PARENTS AND GRANDPARENTS

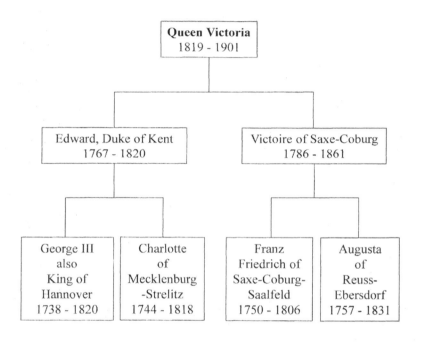

3. THE ROYAL RACE FOR THE BRITISH CROWN

**The four babies born in spring 1819, showing
the dates of their birth and their order in the succession**

Dates of birth	Baby	Order in the succession
26 March	**George of Cambridge**	3rd
27 March	**Charlotte of Clarence**	Died the same day as her birth
24 May	**Victoria of Kent**	1st
27 May	**George of Cumberland**	2nd

The babies' order in the succession was determined by the seniority of their fathers. The duke of Kent was the fourth son of George III; the duke of Cumberland the fifth; and the duke of Cambridge the seventh

4. VICTORIA'S PREDECESSORS

**The Kings of Great Britain
between the time of her birth and her succession to the throne**

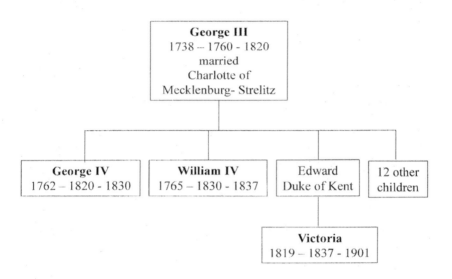

The monarchs of Great Britain are shown in bold with their year of
(1) birth; (2) accession; and (3) death

5. THE FAMILY RELATIONSHIP BETWEEN QUEEN VICTORIA AND PRINCE ALBERT

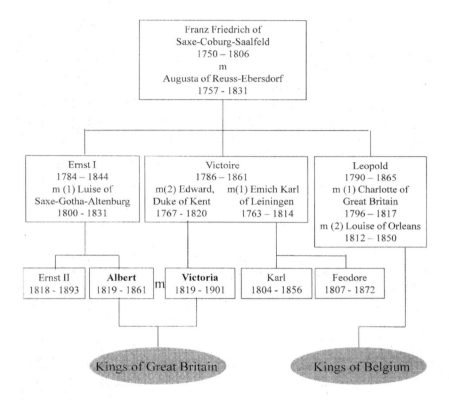

LIST OF ILLUSTRATIONS

All illustrations are from the author's collection

1. The picture I found in the attic – an elderly Queen Victoria in her Golden Jubilee year, after fifty years on the throne (print published by Layfayette and Co, 1887).
2. The young Queen Victoria as a teenager, at the beginning of her reign (Early Victoria print from a drawing by Bouvier).
3. Victoria as a child, in a bonnet with ribbons (*Her Royal Highness the Princess Victoria, August 1828;* engraved by Thomas Wright from a drawing by S Catterson Smith, published May 1829).
4. Princess Charlotte, heiress to the British throne, died in childbirth in November 1817 (print of engraving by William Fry after the 1817 portrait by Sir Thomas Lawrence, published 1907).
5. Victoria's parents – Edward, duke of Kent; and Victoire, princess of Saxe-Coburg (1886 engraving of the duke from the portrait by George Dawe; 1902 print of a drawing of the duchess by Sir George Hayter).
6. The room in Kensington Palace where Victoria was born (print from a photograph by Russell and Sons, 1897).
7. In this early portrait Victoria's status as heiress is indicated by the view of Windsor Castle in the background (lithograph, thought to be Victoria as a young child, from the original picture by W Clerk, published by O Hodgson, early 1820s).
8. Victoria's first name was Alexandrina and this print, from the very beginning of her reign, shows her as Queen Alexandrina (*Her Most Gracious Majesty, Queen Alexandrina Victoria*; print of 1837).
9. Little Drina was brought up in Kensington Palace in London (1902 print from a photo by York and son).
10. Little Drina aged four, dressed in a miniature version of adult clothes and wearing an enormous hat! (Victorian print, from the 1823 painting by S. P. Denning).

11. The heiress to the throne visiting a cotton mill at Belper in Derbyshire (print of a drawing by H. French, 1897).

12. A gorgeous portrait of Victoria with her mother, the duchess of Kent (by Richard James Lane, after the painting by Sir George Hayter; lithograph of 1834).

13. A drawing of Princess Victoria in the 1820s (*The Princess Victoria: Dedicated by permission to Her Royal Highness the Duchess of Kent*; drawn from life by S Catterson Smith, engraved by Richard J Lane, published in the 1820s).

14. The twelve-year-old princess with her governess; a depiction of the moment when Victoria finds out how near she is to the throne (*I see I am near the throne than I thought I was*; print from the drawing by James N. Lee, 1897).

15. Riding a donkey in Kensington Palace Gardens (print from a drawing by H. J. Rhodes, 1897).

16. King William IV (print of 1902).

17. Victoria aged eleven, with sketchbook and pencil (1834 print from an engraving of an 1830 painting by Richard Westall).

18. The new queen; a print published on the day of Victoria's accession (*Queen Victoria* by Richard James Lane; lithograph published on 24 May 1837).

19. Victoria receives the news of her accession (*Your Majesty*, print from the drawing by Mary I. Gow, published by the Berlin Photographic company, 1897).

20. The impression she made at her first Privy Council, on the first day of her reign, was tremendous (*The Queen's First Council*; 1902 print from the 1838 painting by Sir David Wilkie).

21. The Royal Rose of England, in a Spooner's Transformation (*Spooners Transformation No 5, The Royal Rose of* England, published by William Spooner, 1 June 1838).

22. Original invitation to Victoria's coronation in Westminster Abbey.

23 The nineteen-year-old queen, in her coronation regalia (Victorian print from the painting by Sir George Hayter, 1838).

24. The coronation ceremony in Westminster Abbey (antique German print around 1900).
25. A new father figure - the queen and Lord Melbourne out riding at Windsor Castle (*The Queen Riding out with Lord Melbourne*, 1897 print from the painting by Sir Francis Grant).
26. A cartoon about the *Bedchamber Crisis*, when Victoria refused to dismiss any of her Whig ladies (*Childs Play* by John Doyle; lithograph of 14 June 1839).
27. *The Contrast;* this Victorian cartoon from *Spooner of London* favourably compares Victoria to her uncle, the duke of Cumberland (*The Contrast; Victoria (England) and Ernest (Hannover)*, published by W Spooner, 1830s).
28. The young queen charming senior politicians from both the main parties of the day – the Whigs and the Tories (*She Stoops to Conquer; Dedicated to the Queen*, Queen Victoria, Lord Wellington (Tory) and Lord John Russell (Whig), published by J McCormick, 1830s).
29. The Saxe-Coburg candidate for Victoria's hand – Prince Albert at four years old (print of engraving by William Holt from the portrait by Döll, published 1867).
30. Dressed for the evening; the young Victoria loved late nights and parties (lithograph with hand colouring circa 1840).
31. After she came to the throne Victoria enjoyed her new life and independence; dancing at a ball (*A Ball-Room Scene* by John Doyle; lithograph of 3 July 1838).
32. Young Victoria in 1838 (1897 print of portrait by Thomas Sully).
33. Windsor castle, where the cousins, Victoria and Albert, met again in October 1839 (print from the drawing by Henry A. Harper, 1897).
34. Prince Albert at the time of his marriage (1897 print from the 1840 miniature portrait by William Charles Ross).
35. Victoria and Albert were married on 10 February 1840 (*Her Most Gracious Majesty Queen Victoria and His Royal Highness Prince Albert, married 10 February 1840*, engraving by S Bradshaw after a drawing by R W Topham, 1840).

NOTES

1. *The Times* on the day of George IV's funeral – 15 July 1830.
2. *The Times* 20 June 1837.
3. Queen Victoria's journal. RA VIC/MAIN/QVJ (W) Tuesday 20 June 1837 (Princess Beatrice's copies), retrieved 2 January, 2016.
4. Queen Victoria, Cecil Woodham-Smith, page 140.
5. The Greville Diary, entry for 21 June 1837.
6. Street ballad of June 1837; John Johnson Collection, Bodleian Library.
7. Street ballad of January 1840; John Johnson Collection, Bodleian Library.
8. Queen Victoria's journal. RA VIC/MAIN/QVJ (W) Thursday 28 June 1838 (Lord Esher's transcripts), retrieved 2 January, 2016.
9. Thomas Carlyle, 28 June 1837; quoted in Queen Victoria, Helmut and Alison Gernsheim.
10. Queen Victoria's journal. RA VIC/MAIN/QVJ (W) Thursday 10 October 1839 (Princess Beatrice's copies), retrieved 2 January, 2016.
11. Queen Victoria's journal. RA VIC/MAIN/QVJ (W) Friday 11 October 1839 (Lord Esher's transcripts), retrieved 2 January, 2016.
12. Queen Victoria's journal. RA VIC/MAIN/QVJ (W) Tuesday 15 October 1839 (Lord Esher's transcripts), retrieved 2 January, 2016.

SELECTED BIBLIOGRAPHY

The list below includes some of my favourite books and also other sources used for Young Victoria. They are shown in order by date of publication, starting with the earliest.

Sir Herbert Maxwell, *Sixty Years a Queen: The Story of Her Majesty's Reign*. London: Harmsworth Bros Ltd, 1897.

Mrs O F Walton, *Our Gracious Queen, 1837-1897*. London: The Religious Tract Society, 1897.

Mrs Margaret Oliphant, *The Domestic Life of the Queen*. London, Cassell and Company, 1901.

Arthur Benson and Viscount Esher (edited), *The Letters of Queen Victoria: 1837-1861*. London: John Murray, 1908.

Lytton Strachey, *Queen Victoria*. London: Chatto and Windus, 1921.

Philip Whitwell Wilson (edited), *The Greville Diary*. New York: Doubleday, Page and Company, 1927.

Laurence Housman, *Victoria Regina: A Dramatic Biography*. London: Jonathon Cape, 1934.

Roger Fulford, *Royal Dukes: Queen Victoria's 'Wicked Uncles'*. London: Pan Books, 1948.

Helmut and Alison Gernsheim, *Queen Victoria: A Biography in Word and Picture*. London: Longmans, 1959.

Elizabeth Longford, *Victoria RI*. London: Pan Books, 1964.

Cecil Woodham-Smith, *Queen Victoria 1819 – 1861*. London: Hamish Hamilton, 1972.

Jillian Robertson, *The Royal Race for the British Crown 1817 – 1819*. London: Blond and Briggs, 1977.

Daphne Bennett, *King without a Crown*. Philadelphia and New York: J.B. Lippincott Company, 1977.

Christopher Hibbert, *Queen Victoria in her letters and journals: a selection by Christopher Hibbert*. New York: Viking, 1985.

Susan Symons, *The Image of Royalty, Queen Victoria 1837 – 1842*. University of London (Birkbeck College): MA dissertation – unpublished, 1986.

John Wardroper, *Wicked Ernest: The Truth about the Man who was almost Britain's King*. London: Shelfmark Books, 2002.

Queen Victoria's Journals: www.queenvictoriasjournals.org. Windsor: The Royal Archives, 2012.

FASCINATING ROYAL HISTORY

Also published by Roseland Books

Schloss is the German word for castle or palace, and you are never far from one of these in Germany. For most of its history Germany was not a single country but a decentralised federation of independent states, each with its own royal family. These royals were passionate builders and left behind a rich legacy in the thousands of schlösser (the plural of schloss) that cover the German countryside.

Each of these two books by author Susan Symons visits 25 beautiful castles and palaces in Germany and tells the colourful stories of the royal families that built and lived in them. Royalty have always been the celebrities of their day, and these stories from history can rival anything in modern-day television soap operas.

The historical royal stories in the books include the princess from a tiny German state who used her body and her brains to become the ruler of the vast Russian empire; the crown princess who ran away from her husband and six children with their tutor and created a sensation in the international press; and the insignificant princess who was passed on by her fiancé to his brother but who ended up heiress to the throne of England. Two themes emerge from their stories; the lottery of arranged dynastic marriages for royal princesses, and the equally sad fate of their landless younger brothers.

As they lost their ruling families, many of the schlösser went into decline and became prisons, workhouses and other institutions. Some were behind the Iron Curtain for 50 years. The books chart these difficult years and their resurgence and use today as museums, hotels and public buildings.

Schloss and Schloss II are intended to be light-hearted and easy to read; they should appeal to anyone who likes history or travelogues or is interested in people's personal stories.

Many of the schlösser included in the books are not well known to those visiting Germany. If you have not yet been to these wonderful buildings, you are in for a treat.

This book can be seen as an inspiration ... to get out there and find the lesser known palaces and learn more about their history.

Review of Schloss in Royalty Digest Quarterly Journal

Made in the USA
Charleston, SC
25 January 2016